Black & White Photography

12 Secrets to Master the Art of Black and White Photography

James Carren

For more books by this author, please visit
www.photographybooks.us

Table of Contents

Introduction

I've shot a lot of black and white film in my time as a photographer. In fact, I think it may be one of my favorite mediums in all of photography. Of course, this book is about black and white photography as it refers to digital, but when you make that conscious choice to make something black and white in digital, you have to be aware that, to someone, you are going to hearken back to that analog age.

Black and white works differently from color. Inherently, I feel like every photographer worth their salt knows this. But unfortunately, due to knowing this difference, I feel like a lot of photographers make excuses for poor black and white work by saying things like: "The composition was better in color", or "I pushed my ISO all the way up because black and white handles grain better." All I can say to excuses like these is that: 1. If your photograph looks better in color, don't try to make it black and white for the sake of black and white. 2. If your photograph relies solely on color to make it strong, it's not a good photograph and you should probably trash it anyway. 3. Learn how to take a good black and white photo without too much excess grain. This shows technical skill. If for some reason, later, you find that a particular photograph or series calls for excess grain due to conceptual reasons, or looks better that way, then you can aesthetically make that choice, just be aware that you may have to defend it.

Before we get started with learning some good rules on how to make a successful black and white photograph, I want to clarify: When people say that there is no wrong way to make art, they are talking about expression. If you can defend your choices with good reasons, more power to you. But you always want to make sure that your technical skills are sound to begin with. If, at the end of this book, you are still struggling with the principles of black and white or with composing strong photos in black and white, I would truly suggest taking it all the way back to analog to learn. Sometimes, the completely different mindset can really help to cause a shift in thinking and make things easier.

Deciding Whether or Not to Shoot in Black and White

As I stated in my introduction, your photo should never, ever, rely solely on color. When you do decide to make use of color in a photograph, you should use it to your advantage and have knowledge of how color will affect the mood of your viewer. You should control how they view your photo, and color is a huge tool. At the same time, knowing when *not* to use color is also a huge tool. You should never make the choice arbitrarily, because you think it should be one or the other. What does the photo or series itself call for?

This, to me, is the tricky part, because as an analog photographer, I am very aware of when I have black and white film loaded into my camera and when I don't. When you know you are shooting in black and white, it does something to your brain, where you begin to consciously consider the things around you in terms of grey scale. With training and practice, you know which colors will translate to which grey tone. But on the other hand, the benefit of shooting in digital as most of you will be, is that you can shoot all your photos in color and then have the option to have both color and black and white versions, because some photos do happen to look great in both. However, if you are going out with the intention of shooting black and white, you should bear that in mind even while looking at color versions in the back of your monitor.

So when are some times that you should choose to shoot in black and white? Everyone really has their own personal reasons, but here are some of my own:

- You don't want any distractions. Some people like a lot of color, and that's just fine. But if you've already got a particularly chaotic scene going on and you want the chaos to be present but not overwhelming, you might choose to shoot in black and white. Black and white can also be a particular help if you find the general scene is drawing attention away from your subject. By reducing everything to black, white, and grey, the brain is more easily able to focus on content.

- You just don't like the colors in a scene you shot, but the scene itself is awesome. I'm really big on color theory, and thus on using color to control the perceptions of your viewer. If you set up all your own shots in a studio, then you should be able to always only get the colors you want in a photo. However, most of us go out and walk around to take at least some of our photos, or we get hired and thrown into situations, such as weddings, where our color palettes have largely been chosen for us. So in that case, you can eliminate a distasteful palette by using black and white.

- The photo has boring colors. You can also use black and white to inject a little bit more drama into a strong photo that's flat when it comes to color.

- The photo is very based on shape and line. If you want to make your photo even more geometric, clean, or simple, reducing it to black and white can do that. This works especially well with things like detail close ups of architecture.

Tonal Differences and Contrast

The cool thing about black and white is that you have so many options, and I'm actually not sure a lot of new photographers realize that. I think some people have this perception of black and white being a one look thing, and that's probably because when most people start out with black and white, they want everything to be dramatic and punchy. Don't get me wrong, dramatic and punchy is definitely a valid choice on some occasions, but you don't want to default to it. What I would suggest is that when you do your first black and white series, you go ahead and get that out of your system. Meaning, shoot it, and then crank everything up. Crank up your ISO before you shoot, and make everything super high contrast in post. You know you want to, and speaking from experiences I've had, I know you will. But after that first series, put it behind you, and realize that black and white is a lot more subtle and versatile than you at first gave it credit for.

In your second series, you might want to try going very, very soft. By this I mean, let there be only small tonal changes in the scenes you're photographing and in the way you're working with the photo in post. By doing this, you will definitely find which aesthetic you lean more towards, and you may find that you actually dislike both extremes. But by exploring both, you can more easily work towards something in the middle that becomes your own aesthetic.

Even after you think you've found an aesthetic that's pleasing to you, don't get stuck in it. With each body of work that you make, you should ask yourself, "What does this photo require? Is it supposed to be soft and ethereal, or does it need to hit my viewer over the head?" If you don't know the answer, consider your content. What is the photo about? What do you want your viewer to feel?

Also remember that dark and light are different from high and low contrast. Consider where your shadows and light are, and where you want the focus to be, because believe it or not, your mindset really affects how you shoot, and then subsequently develop something. Your psyche is a vital part of the artwork, and you'll notice how it changes as you go through different stages in your life.

Experimenting with shooting and printing can open you up to new possibilities as an artist, and can also help you change up older photos dramatically, into new and exciting works of art.

Being Technically Competent

As a photographer, I try to read a lot about what other photographers are doing and how they do their work. Everyone has their own philosophy, and I have nothing but respect for that, whether you're self-taught, or, like me, went to school to learn your craft. But one of the biggest things I learned in school that I feel like self-taught photographers are often lacking is technical competence.

Technical competence is what separates professional photographers from amateurs, and while I do understand that it can be hard to learn and understand all the numbers and math that goes with it, once you do learn it, it will become second nature to you.

The reason I bring this up is because, recently, I was reading about black and white craft, and there was a photographer who said that ISO does not matter when it comes to black and white because black and white can handle much more grain than color can. This is true because you can definitely clean up noise in black and white much more easily. Tonally, grey tones are closer to each other than colors are, so when you clean it up you aren't going to get funky color shifts in the same way because the colors aren't going to get dragged around into each other. However, if noise isn't something that you want, you shouldn't just leave your ISO cranked up to something ridiculous. And in fact, if noise isn't something that you feel directly affects how your viewers are going to perceive your photo (as in, it adds something you feel is essential) then shoot it on an ISO that is "normal" for the photo.

ISO, or ASA, comes straight from analog photography and refers to the speed of the film. Slow ISOs, such as 100 or 200, are going to produce images that are smooth and low grain, where ISO 800 would have quite a bit of grain. With digital cameras, you can push it up even higher. I think my camera (which is quite outdated, unfortunately) goes up to 3200, with newer models pushing absolutely ridiculous numbers. What fast films (or high ISOs as the case may be) do is allow you to get more light in the film essentially. So if you're shooting in the dark, you're probably going to need a really high ISO in order to see what's going on if you don't have any other light source. But this will inevitably result in grain, and I don't care what anyone says, even if black and white grain is less distracting and/or easier to handle, that doesn't mean that it looks good or that you should use it simply for the sake of being edgy.

To be on the safe side and really make sure that I'm getting the information I want to get, I generally will shoot with ISO 400 film. This also means that generally, my ISO on my digital is around 400, for your typical indoor scene. It's an ISO that's smack in the middle of the general range which is why it works so well. Of course, with a digital camera you'll be able to tell pretty quickly whether it's working or not, and to adjust accordingly. If you really want that intense grainy look, I would suggest shooting one frame on a normalized ISO and one on a high one. That way, if you change your mind later, you've got choices. I would also suggest using equivalent exposures to vary how much movement, or lack thereof, that you have in your image. This can change your perception of your image just as much as varying contrast can.

Pay Attention to the Light

This may seem like a no-brainer, but I still feel the need to reiterate it. Photographs are made because of light, so you would think this would be the one rule you wouldn't forget. The amount of photos I see taken in bad lighting, however, seem to say otherwise.

With black and white, as we have discussed, everything gets pared down to the minimal. It's less distracting; it can be more austere. Without color, it's harder to hide your mistakes, which is why I feel so many amateur photographers lean on color as a crutch.

When you go to take your photos, pay attention not only to the subject you're photographing, but also to the light conditions surrounding your subject. Since black and white really has the ability to reduce everything down to pure shape if you let it, consider the light a part of it. After all, the way light and shadows fall on and interact with your subject can also create shape. You also want the light to be pleasing on the subject, although with black and white I feel like you have more freedom to make use of some extreme chiaroscuro.

Experiment with areas of deep dark and light, and see how the grey scale reduces things down to pure geometry. I'll be continuing with this concept in my next chapters.

Texture

Some people think that texture is more important in black and white than it is in color, while I am of the opinion that I love it in everything. However, as with lighting, I do feel that in black and white it can be very important, especially if you want to do conceptual abstract work. Your choice of textures, or lack thereof, if you choose, make an integral statement about your work. Texture can even be the entirety of a picture if you want it to be.

Texture can also be important when you have a picture that is made up largely of lighter tones, those close to white, or of darker shades, those closer to black. When you have a picture that has a very limited tonal range, things can begin to blend into each other, which can be cool, but you also want some variation for interest. This is where texture comes in.

You may have noticed that in still life shoots, black fabric is often used to set objects on. That fabric is almost always artfully draped in such a way to show texture. This helps to differentiate it from the background or backdrop, especially if it's the same color.

Also keep in mind when shooting black and white that similar colors are going to show up as similar tones. So if you have red apples in a slightly darker red bowl, bear in mind that you'll have to push your development to really get a difference, even if the apples have, say, a little bit of yellow, where it might look like very obviously different reds in color. Also, the yellow might show up as a similar grey tone, so bear that in mind as you prepare to do post processing. You can push one channel more than the other if you like. To use texture in this situation to differentiate between apple and bowl, you may consider using a textured bowl, such as one with a circular pitted pattern or wood grain. The lack of smoothness will catch the light differently, giving differing tonalities in places. You could also choose to use the apple itself, by cutting it up and allowing the inner texture of the fruit to show.

Use the wrinkling technique when working with models as well. Black on black and white on white both look really interesting, but you don't want everything to blend into everything else. If your model is just wearing a plain black or white shirt, try wrinkling it a little bit, or having them pose in such a way that wrinkles occur in the fabric naturally. Or, if you have the choice of clothing your model, put them in something differently textured from the smoothness of the backdrop, such as a beaded gown or a leather jacket. That's really all you need, and texture generates so much interest that you don't need it to be over the top.

Have fun and experiment . . . see how little or how much texture you can put into a photograph that has a similar tonal range throughout. And when shooting portraits, perhaps don't *just* stick with a plain white backdrop. Things like wood and brick can look especially edgy in black and white.

Composition

I am a firm believer that composition is important no matter the medium, format, or absence or presence of color. Too often, new photographers will use color as a crutch. And while color can be an important component of a photograph, it needs to be used, or not used, wisely and to your advantage. If you have chosen to use black and white, as I'm assuming if you are reading this, then you have your reasons. You know that it pares everything down to the minimal, and you also know that it removes color as a distraction. It can also be an aesthetic consideration. Black and white, even if done digitally, can help to remove time period from a photo. This is part of what I mean when I say that the medium pares a photo down to its bare bones. It removes all the excess considerations. And because of this, it's especially necessary that your composition be very strong.

Use all of the elements of composition to your favor, including even color. Some of the elements you'll want to consider are: Rule of thirds, leading lines, weight, juxtaposition, depth, orientation, balance, tension, color, framing, shape. I'll just give you a quick run down of each term, as well as how you would apply it in a photograph.

- **Rule of thirds**: The rule of thirds is typically the first rule learned in a lot of college art classes. Basically, you take a photo and you divide it into 9 squares using two vertical lines and two horizontal lines. The goal is to make sure that the main part of your composition doesn't fall in the middle square, which would make a picture stagnant and boring in most instances. Ideally, you want the main points of interest to fall along one or more of the lines' intersections. It's also fine if they fall within the edges of squares. The rule of thirds will help you break down the misconceived notion that things should always be perfectly centered, because rarely is that the case.

- **Leading line**: Leading lines, and also eye lines, are existing or inferred lines that occur within a photo. Now, just because there happens to be a line in your photo doesn't necessarily mean that it's a leading line. You want to use those lines within the composition to guide the eye of the viewer through and around the photo, and to the most important part of the photo. Thus, you have to be careful with your framing to ensure that things like paths or rows of things end up in the right position to have importance to the photo and not to just stop the eye suddenly, which can kill your photo. Eye lines are kind of like leading lines, but they are implied, and more often than not, they are made when the eyes of two subjects meet, or if the eyes of a subject are drawn elsewhere in the photo. This also helps to guide the eye of the viewer.

- **Weight**: Weight happens because of where you place a subject, or subjects, in the frame. No matter what, your photo is going to have weight, but you want to place it in such a way that it has meaningful impact. This correlates with the rule of thirds very well. Weight can also be achieved by the way you print the border. For example, bottom weighted frames look very good and professional.

- **Juxtaposition**: Juxtaposition is where you have two things side by side that are opposites to each other. Now, in a photo, side by side can be split via the rule of thirds any way you want it to. This can be a consideration of symbolic content, or a consideration of visual differentiation. It's all up to you what you consider to be juxtaposition, as long as you can defend it.

- **Depth**: Consider whether you want your composition to have a shallow depth of field, meaning that only the things in the foreground are in focus at its shallowest, or a deep depth of field, where everything from foreground to background is in focus and tack sharp. Of course, there are variations in between these two extremes, and what you choose is an aesthetic choice that's up to you. As you select your depth of field, consider whether tack sharp or dreamy and shallow would best serve the purpose of your photograph. No matter the depth of field you choose, you should also consider what's going on in all depths of the photo, including the mid-ground, which many people forget about.

- **Orientation**: As you are composing a photo, think about whether you want it to be horizontal or vertical. A lot of photographers do have a preferred orientation that they naturally shoot a lot without realizing it. While this is okay, it's also good to have some variety in your shots. If you shoot abstract photography, it might be interesting to rotate your photographs all the way around to see which composition is the most interesting after you've shot it. You can also do this with photos that aren't abstract, to be experimental.

- **Balance**: Balance is very important to a photo, but contrary to popular belief, balance doesn't necessarily mean that things have to be symmetrical. In fact, often, groups of odd numbers, or asymmetry, can be more aesthetically appealing than even numbers, because it creates more interest and tension. That isn't to say that symmetry can't work, especially if it's framing the edges of a picture, it just needs to be done sparingly and with purpose.

- **Tension:** Tension can be created by using the elements I've already mentioned in such a way that it creates interest in the photograph. Tension can be caused by appropriate framing of a scene that inherently has tension, such as a fight or the moment before a kiss. It can also be caused by the intersection of lines and shapes, by the drama of chiaroscuro, by the collision of complementary colors, or by the confusion or discomfort often caused by two juxtaposed elements.

- **Color:** Despite the fact that this is a book about black and white photography, you still need to pay attention to color in your composition. This is because different colors show up as different tonalities of grey in black and white. So you wouldn't want to photograph a scene with very similar colors necessarily, although that can still be an artistic consideration too.

- **Framing:** Framing refers to how you choose to place your subject within the frame. With people, you always want to make sure that all limbs are present within the frame. Even when you visually cut off body parts in photos, it can make your audience very uncomfortable.

- **Shape:** Pay attention to existing shapes within a frame, especially if they repeat. Look for things like circles and triangles, but also for more complex shapes. You can also use your subjects to create shapes of interest for your audience. This kind of thought process will come to you more as you learn to pay attention to the rules of composition.

Headshots

In order to take good black and white headshots, you will be following a lot of the rules I've already discussed within this book. However, I will try to reiterate them specifically for headshots here.

So why, specifically, do people choose to have black and white headshots taken? I would say that it's really because they're classy and timeless. Too much or too vibrant color can be a distraction, especially if the headshots are for a professional purpose, such as for an actor to send to agencies. They are also cheaper to print because color ink tends to cost more.

While you can choose to use black and white for these sensible reasons, there is also the matter of aesthetic choice. There are many reasons why you might artistically choose to use black and white. If you are a documentary photographer, it can be a good choice because it removes distractions from a scene which is unscripted and which may already be filled with distractions. It allows you to focus on the meat of what is going on.

Again, it also makes something timeless. If you are careful with attire, you can actually convince the viewer that they don't know what time period a picture is from. While I don't feel that it so much *enhances* detail, I feel that it does make the viewer focus on detail and texture because you don't have the sensory input of color.

Black and white can also make for a much more dramatic headshot if you play off of your deep darks in the shadows.

All that said, I do believe that if you are shooting digitally, you should always provide your client with the option of having their images in black and white or color, or both if they request it. Never get rid of your original color RAW files.

Now, what, specifically, should you pay attention to when shooting black and white headshots? Well, you want to make it interesting, so there are a few ways you can do this. Use the elements of your photo to create interest. You have your lighting, your background, and your texture.

Play around with your lighting. Whatever you have available to you, you can use to make headshots creative, whether that's just one light or five. Try to start out with a typical two light setup if you can, one to light the background and one as a hair or rim light near your subject's head. You'll have to set it up differently for each client that you have, as it's dependent on height. Using flash or not is really up to you.

As for background, you can either choose to use a traditional seamless in white, or you can opt for black, which is just as clean but a little bit edgier. You can also find seamlesses in any other color under the sun, but for the purposes of black and white, the only other one I would really consider might be a soft grey. I've heard some photographers say that a plain seamless is boring for a black and white headshot, and honestly, you may think it is, and it may in fact be. But if it's what your client needs or requests, then it's what you should use. If it's all up to aesthetic consideration, and all you have available to you is your seamless, here's something you might want to try, and it's actually a bit tricky to do. Try shooting white on a white seamless, or black on a black seamless. With a portrait, just have your subject wear that color. Especially when you prepare it in black and white, it's going to take a lot of skill to make sure that you achieve some degree of separation. It's all in the lighting and post, although you do want to try to get as much in camera as you can.

In order to get separation, you also want to try to integrate texture in the fabric of the shirt your subject is wearing. This shouldn't be a problem as long as there is some tension in their pose.

If you have the license to use a background other than a seamless, you might want to try something like wood, brick, or even graffiti or a patterned seamless, if it wouldn't be too distracting. If you use wood or brick, which both have natural variations in color, you will have some tonality changes behind your subject, which adds interest.

All in all, you want to make sure that you take a good, solid headshot that would look good either way, because if it's a strong picture, both you and your client will be happy.

Post Processing

Post processing in black and white really isn't that different than it is for color, except that saturation doesn't really factor in so much. When you take your color RAW file into either Photoshop or Lightroom, make sure that you save a color version before you convert it into black and white. Also make sure that you do convert it to black and white and not to grey scale. When you convert to grey scale, though it may look the same, the algorithm throws away the color channel information, which you're going to need in order to process the photo the way you want to.

When you convert to black and white, Photoshop will automatically bring up the default color controls. There are other presets you can choose from to help get you in the ballpark of the look you want, but again, these are just starting points. You'll want to fine tune for yourself using the sliders.

Here's something to watch out for with black and white though: don't just push your blacks up all the way and push your contrast. Often, when photographers start shooting in black and white, they want everything to look edgy. My suggestion would be to go ahead and do it; get it out of your system. Then, as you move on with your work, you should really try to consider what the photo itself calls for. Consider how you want your audience to feel as they look at your work and edit for that. If you don't know how you want your audience to feel, then try editing the photo several ways. If you think that all black and white looks similar, then you haven't seen a lot of different edits.

Aside from the color channel considerations, your editing is going to be very similar. You need to clean up dust, scratches and any other blemishes that may have been on your lens at the time you shot. If you are editing a portrait, you need to do all the basic retouching that you would do normally: clean up blemishes and redness, smooth out skin, possibly apply a softening filter. I would suggest that you make your edits before you convert to black and white just to make it easier to see what you're doing. And don't scrimp; imperfections will definitely show up on a finished piece. If you would like to leave in grain from a high ISO for aesthetic purposes, it's fine to do so, as long as you can defend it. However, I would never suggest leaving flecks of dust all over your image. I find that a lot of new photographers think that this is okay to do in a black and white image because they think that it makes the image look "vintage." Dust, however, is never going to do that. It's just going to make your images look sloppy and unprofessional. Most likely, the reason people think that it's okay to leave dust on black and white images is because they often see it on old film strips. However, if you do see this, it's a result of bad practices. It's due to the film and/or the scanner not being properly cleaned of dust before scanning.

If You're Struggling . . .

Now, this is a less than traditional technique, and is not true black and white. However, I feel like it might be a technique that could help new photographers stop being so dependent on color and saturation. Obviously, we cannot see in black and white, but my idea is this. Set a day or night (or both) that you can go out and shoot with the purpose of looking to make color photographs that look black and white. This doesn't mean that everything in the scene necessarily has to be either black or white. Look for variations of grey and desaturated colors as well.

The reason I say to also shoot at night is because the dark provides a natural kind of desaturation, tamping colors down to look like maybe just a shade or tint of their former vibrance.

As with everything else, I'd say to look for scenes that already somewhat fool the eye in camera. It doesn't really count so much if you just take it into Photoshop later and mess with it. I believe that this exercise will make a photographer of any skill and experience level think, and push their boundaries.

Additionally, you could leave these as color as a cool kind of trick for your audience, or you can convert them into black and white and see if they are any stronger than your initial photos. This exercise may actually help you to start "thinking" for black and white, so to speak. You can't think in black and white, but you can begin to disregard the power of the color on your monitor to consider what the needs of a black and white image are. And you do have the advantage over black and white film photographers, of being able to see your image as you shoot instead of after you've developed it.

If you are still struggling with black and white compositions after trying this, there are two more things I can suggest.

The first is actually the direct opposite of advice in the first chapter, which is to always shoot in color. Now, I will temper this by saying that for any professional shoot or shoot for your portfolio, you should always shoot in color to preserve the integrity of the image. But as an exercise, try the black and white setting on your camera. That way, you can see what your image looks like already processed as black and white. Just be careful never to leave your camera on that setting.

My second suggestion would be to actually go and shoot and develop black and white film. There is just something about how work intensive that process is that makes everyone into a better photographer. Over time, you also learn how to see what your camera sees without being able to see the finished product. Of course, there will always be surprises, but that's part of the fun.

Conclusion

Digital black and white photography is a lot different from traditional black and white analog photography, but as I have shown, it does have some things in common. Hopefully this book has helped you as you choose to expand your portfolio with a black and white section, and hopefully your clients love having that option as well.

Remember that taking a good black and white photo isn't so different from taking a good photo in general, but do remember that process of the black and white photo itself has different needs.

Remember that your first step is to consider if and why you need to shoot a black and white photo in the first place. As long as you can defend your reasons, you're good to go.

Then, you need to pay attention to tonal differences and contrast. Often, new photographers think that color doesn't matter in a scene, but it still does, and so does how you choose to later develop the image. Not all black and white looks the same.

Make sure you pay attention to the light and to all the elements of composition, so that you have an image that is worthy of, and can stand up to, being black and white.

Did you Like "Black & White Photography"?

Before you go, I'd like to say thank you so much for purchasing my book.

I know you could have picked from dozens of books on this subject, but you took a chance with mine, and I'm truly grateful for that.

So, once again, a big thanks for downloading this book and reading all the way to the end—I truly appreciate it.

Now I'd like to ask for a small favor if you don't mind:

Would you be so kind as to take a minute of your time and leave a review for this book on Amazon?

This feedback will help me continue to write the kind of books that help you get results. And if you loved it, then please feel free to let me know! :)

More Books by James Carren

Portrait Photography - 9 Tips Your Camera Manual Never Told You About Portrait Photography

Landscape Photography - 10 Essential Tips to Take Your Landscape Photography to The Next Level

Photography Lighting - Top 10 Must-Know Photography Lighting Facts to Shoot Like a Pro in Your Home Studio

Photography For Beginners - From Beginner To Expert Photographer In Less Than a Day!

Photography Business: 20 Things You Need to Know Before Starting a Successful Photography Business

Photoshop – Master The Basics: Top 12 Easy Photoshop Tips and Tricks for Beginners

Photoshop – Master The Basics 2: 9 Techniques to Take Your Photoshop Skills to The Next Level

www.ingramcontent.com/pod-product-compliance
Lightning Source LLC
Chambersburg PA
CBHW070752180526
45168CB00004B/1592